PIZZA & CHOIR

A walk through the garden of life
that leads you home.

REBECCA MOORE

Pizza & Choir
Copyright 2019 ©Rebecca Moore

Published by Star Label Publishing
P.O. Box 1511, Buderim, QLD, Australia
publishing@starlabel.com.au

Cover art: Tony Moore
Cover photography: Cartia Christie and Jsjiah Moore

1st Edition January 2019
2nd Edition July 2025
All rights reserved. No part of this publication may be reproduced in any form; stored in a retrieval system; or transmitted; or used in any other form; or by any other means without prior written permission of the publisher (except for brief quotes for the purpose of review or promotion).

All Scripture quotations unless otherwise indicated are from The Holy Bible, New International Version®, NIV® Copyright © 1973, 1978, 1984, 2011 by Biblica, Inc.™ Used by permission. All rights reserved worldwide.

Scripture quotations marked (ESV) are from The Holy Bible, English Standard Version® (ESV®), copyright © 2001 by Crossway, a publishing ministry of Good News Publishers. Used by permission. All rights reserved.

The views expressed here-in remain the sole responsibility of the author, who exempts the publisher from all liability. The author and publisher do not assume responsibility for any loss, damage, or disruption caused by the contents, errors or omissions, whether such contents, errors, or omissions result from opinion, negligence, accident, or any other cause, and hereby disclaim any and all liability to any party.

ISBN: 978-0-6484602-0-6

DEDICATION

This book is dedicated to my husband Tony, who selflessly gives to encourage me, to motivate me and to redirect me when I get distracted.

To my four incredibly entertaining children whom I adore, who supply me with inspiration and make life so very interesting.

To our parents for their enduring love, encouragement and support and who graciously seem to enjoy the constant stream of stories sent their way.

And to my wonderful supportive readers, friends and family. May you always find a quiet place to read a book and rest.

Most importantly, this book is dedicated to the One I write for, who fills me with His abundant words whenever I ask and wait on Him, and who walks with me each
and every day
—to my wonderful Saviour and friend,
Jesus Christ.

CONTENTS

DEDICATION	iii
CONTENTS	iv
ACKNOWLEDGEMENTS	vi
PREFACE	vii

SUMMER TIME

Pizza And Choir	1
That Moment When...	5
Running On Empty	11
Good Samaritans	15
Poem – The Traveller	21
Lifestyle App That Does Everything—If Only!	27
Spiderman Or Not?	31
Hold That Boat!	35

AUTUMN

	41
Let's Get Real – Mother's Day Mash-Up	43
That Was Not My Intention	47
Removing The Spirit Of Heaviness	51
Poem—The Winds Of Change	57
Road Maps And Detours	63
I Could've Kicked Myself!	67
A Walk In The Rain	71

WINTER	75
The God Of The Hills And Valleys	77
Poem – They Met In The Park With The Leaves	83
Not Finished Yet	89
How To Get Off A Ski Lift	95
Poem – Fiery Chariots	101
Look Out For The Bowling Balls	105
Word-Planting	111
SPRING	117
Yes My Darling, You Will Fly	119
Awaiting Beauty	123
Poem – The Garden	129
"Squark!" Is Not The Sound A Car Should Make	133
Soccer Mums And Welcome Distractions	137
Poem – The Star That Saw The World	145
Life Is Good	151
Don't Be Afraid Of Something New	155
AFTERWORD	**159**
ABOUT THE AUTHOR	**161**
ALSO BY REBECCA MOORE	**162**

ACKNOWLEDGEMENTS

I'd like to thank my husband, Tony Moore, for his constant love, encouragement and determination in guiding me to reach my dreams. You never cease to believe in me and I am forever grateful to God for bringing us together.

To our beautiful children Cartia, Jsjiah, Benaton, and Summer for your love and patience – especially when I read each story out loud to see if it still sounds good outside of my head.

To my mum, Jennifer Peterson – my first-go-to-editor. Thank you for sharing your love of English, spelling and all things grammar with me, and for your continual guidance, love and support. You are a bright and shining gem.

To my dad, Alan Peterson, for your wise counsel, endless love and for planting the wonderful gift of stories and imagination in my heart from an early age. I'll always be grateful.

I'd like to thank my editor, David Goodwin, for the time and effort you have put into giving this book the final polishing it needed.

Thank you also to Christian Today Australia; The Salvation Army's Warcry Magazine; The Australian Christian Channel and the Encounter Magazine, amongst others, for publishing my stories, articles and reviews over the years.

I also dedicate this book to all those who feel they go unheard. I started writing because I could rarely get a word in!

PREFACE

The gum trees soar to the left and right of my view of the distant mountains, the mist nestled in the valley looks like snow.

Our animals graze on the dew-glistened hill while the birds with their morning song, swoop down to catch the early worm. This is the view from my desk as I sit to write my stories. Picturesque and serene.

Yet this hasn't always been so. The journey so far has been as bumpy as the hills and valleys I see before me. Each bump, just like the seasons, has taught me something, equipping me for life, increasing my endurance, and teaching perseverance which has brought me to the place I am today. I feel blessed, not because of what lies before me but because of what I have overcome, equipping me for what lies ahead.

I've learnt that beauty is not just in the easy times, but in the process of growing – the good and the bad together. That's where Pizza and Choir has come from. Not from highly academic insights into psychology or the like (though they are there), but rather in the everydayness of life that we all experience, as we take moments to laugh, even at ourselves, to inspire happiness and to bring joy. Without the valleys there are no mountains and when both mountains and valleys exist, the view is much more satisfying.

Pizza and Choir has been divided into four seasons, dappled with poetry. With each season comes change and each change carries a beauty uniquely its own – to be enjoyed and valued.

Each story is short enough to easily read over a cup of coffee in the hope of giving encouragement and also as a reminder that God is interested in our today, the season we are in right now.

The poetry woven throughout this book is an echo of a moment in each season. My hope is that we fearlessly find the joy in each moment of life that we are currently in for, though our walk may feel lonely at times, we never truly walk alone.

In love, I'm stopping now to go and smell some roses.

SUMMER TIME

—harsh, long and hot; filled with fun activities, mostly involving water to cool us down, yet the hot weather continues for a large part of our year, often leaving us feeling drained and looking forward to the cooler months which seem to come and go far too quickly.

PIZZA AND CHOIR

 t was drawing towards the end of the six week Christmas holidays.

My children were aged three, four, ten and eleven at the time, and the house had echoed with childish noises for many days.

That's fine for the most part, but on this particular day my ears were tired and I needed a rest. I could hear my children calling for me, but knowing more food wasn't as urgent as they made it out to be, I closed myself in my room to take some much needed 'me' time.

Me time—shmee time
Within a few minutes, my three-year-old, with her gorgeous cluster of ringlets circling the base of her head, bounced into my room and announced: "Mummy, da kids want you!"

"Well," I replied, "you tell *da kids* that Mummy just wants some peace and quiet."

Her little eyes lit up and she bolted from my room almost excitedly – which I thought was strange.

She then poised herself on our back deck, cupped her chubby little hands around her mouth and, at the top of her three-year-old voice, called out to the neighbourhood, "Evi-body! Mummy wants some pizza and choir!"

Not quite what I meant, but hey – that could work too. The excitement at this point required me to put aside my 'quiet-time' and head to the kitchen to see what food I could find – preferably in the form of pizza. The choir sounded from the back yard in the form of cheers when the food was brought out.

Jesus knows
I love that when we mums get tired, Jesus understands us. He knows well the demands of feeding His children.

Matthew chapter 14 tells us of John the Baptist's death. On the news of this, Jesus needed some time to be by Himself.

'When Jesus heard what had happened, he withdrew by boat privately to a solitary place.' —Matthew chapter 14 verse 13

Before long, He was followed by crowds who were eager to be with Him. Jesus had compassion on them, spoke to them, healed them and then fed them – five thousand of them! He took care of His 'children' who ate until they were satisfied.

Still needing rest, Jesus dismissed the crowd and sent the disciples on ahead, then went up on a mountainside by Himself to pray. After a time of refreshment with His Father, he was then able to meet the disciples again as He walked to them on the water in the early hours of the morning.

Recharge and refresh others
Recharging renews us, allowing us to be able to refresh others. Spending time with our Heavenly Father fills us so that we are then able to help and look after those around us.

We are wrapped up in these human bodies that fail us and get tired and weary, but our Father in Heaven knows just what we need – we need to be still and spend time with Him.

So, take time to be revived. Fill yourself with the Word, worship, and nourishment – food for the soul as well as the body. And if that comes in the form of pizza and choir – so be it.

THAT MOMENT WHEN ...

My young friends on social media often begin their posts with the phrase: *That moment when...*

This is usually followed by something awkward that has happened to them or something obvious which has dawned on them such as *'That moment when you realise you've turned up to work with two different socks on'* or similar.

Well, I have a few of my own:

That moment when ... you try to elegantly enter the water in your swimming costume for the first time in Summer, and then get pummelled by the first wave, resurfacing with your hair smothered across your face, smacked by sand and gasping for air.

That moment when ... you turn up to a friend's BBQ in an A-line cotton dress and stand on their high deck on a windy day only to find you can't see your friend while they are talking to you because your dress is in the air!

That moment when ... your friend says happy birthday to you and you say happy birthday back to them and it's not even their birthday.

And I could go on, but I think that's enough embarrassment for one day. You may or may not relate. Hopefully I'm not the only one who has things like this happen to them – I think I can safely say I'm not and that there must be at least one other person out there.

Just laugh
When I was younger, these kind of moments would have left me *dying from embarrassment,* as the saying goes. But I find as I celebrate more birthdays, my reactions to these situations are different.

My first reaction, of course, is blood-draining-from-my-face shock but following that mini-moment, my reaction is to burst into laughter, (laughing with myself, of course, not at myself) and – when I think about it again later – to laugh some more.

In my first example, when I resurfaced from the pummeling wave, I was comforted by the hysterical laughter of my husband. I imagined how ridiculous it must have looked and was really glad I had been able to entertain him, and therefore I joined in with his laughter (making a mental note not to hold back my laughter next time something similar happens to him).

Falling short

When we think about how we were created, it is actually a blessing to have faults. So many times I fall short of my expectations. In a perfect world, I would never offend anyone; I would be available to attend every invitation; I would remember every special date (and to write it on the calendar); I would remember people's names (especially when introducing them to others); I would have a perfect variety of meals every night of the week and my house would be immaculately clean.

But it's not like that. And, although it is not my intention, I probably let people down more than I would like to and that makes me sad. But, when I stop to think about it, I realise I should probably be a little easier on myself.

So many times, I wish I could master everything and be done with it, but when I stop and see that those close to me actually love me with all my faults (and even draw entertainment from them) I realise that kind of love is a beautiful thing – it's comforting and reassuring. That kind of love is called unconditional love.

Unconditional love

There are so many things to thank God for, but right near the top of my list would have to be that He loves us unconditionally. Firstly, He made us, so He loves us immediately without us even having to do anything. Secondly, He knows we're not perfect and gave the gift that He is always working on us to create who He made us to be.

I love the story in the Bible about the woman who washed Jesus' feet in expensive perfume. She had lived a life of sin and was so grateful to Jesus for His forgiveness that she wept and kissed His feet while washing them. This upset the owner of the house but, after explaining to him the reason behind this woman's gratefulness for forgiveness, Jesus simply said:

"Therefore her sins – and they are many – are forgiven, for she loved me much; but one who is forgiven little, shows little love." —Luke chapter 7 verse 47

Faults and all
If we were created perfect, we would have no need for God. We would have no appreciation for the forgiveness He offers, and we would have no love for the One who created us because we would be self-sufficient. Knowing our humanness, and being aware of our temporary state on this earth, makes what Jesus did for us so very amazing and life-giving.

Jesus saved us. He actually saved us from ourselves and the more we realise our shortcomings, the more we can love the One who saved us, knowing He loves us regardless of what we've done or how many times we embarrass ourselves.

So, next time you do something embarrassing, remember that we are fearfully and wonderfully made and thank Jesus that He loves us – faults and all.

RUNNING ON EMPTY

It was a busy school morning. I managed to get the kids out the door but with only minutes to spare.

As all four children bundled into the car, I turned the engine on only to have the petrol light appear on my dashboard! The petrol was low – very low.

With only minutes to spare, I had two choices.

One: I could stop on the way to school to get petrol but this would mean the kids running late;

or

Two: I could take the risk and drive straight to the school and hope to high heaven there would be enough petrol to get me there.

A decision must be made
Time was running short and I had to make a quick decision. As I approached the fork in the road, I decided to take the road to the left and head straight to the school. We'd had enough late slips, and today was not going to be another one.

The children arrived just on time – no late slip necessary. Breathing a sigh of relief, I waved the children off with a cheesy mum smile, and drove out of the school carpark giving myself a mental pat on the back. *Best mum ever!*

As I performed a U-turn to head back to the motorway, something happened. My car stopped midway through the turn, leaving me stranded diagonally across the right hand lane on the bend of a road. *This is awkward.*

As I retrieved my phone from my handbag to call my husband, some nice people pulled over to help me. Together we pushed my car to the side of the road out of harm's way, and it was not long after that my hero-husband arrived with enough petrol to get me to the nearest station.

Sometimes we think we can make it – but on what fuel?
As relieved as I was that the children had made it to school on time, I didn't have what I needed to get to where I was going. Sometimes we think we can make it in our own strength but when it comes down to it, our own strength will only get us so far. The warning signs were there, and there was a solution that would see me last the distance, but I ignored it and suffered the consequences.

PIZZA AND CHOIR

Sometimes in life we push things to the limit when we should, and do, know better. I should have been better prepared, I should have refueled when the warning light first appeared on my dashboard the day before. I should have pushed the kids out the door 20 minutes earlier. I should have ... I should have ...

There are many things we should have done, and in hindsight it all makes perfect sense. But in the moment, we're pushed for time, we're distracted by circumstance and we're focused on other things when what we really need to be doing is refueling.

The water that never runs dry
In John chapter 4, we read about a Samaritan woman who had spent years running from one relationship to another. Rejected by others because of her lifestyle, she collected water from the well at noon, most likely because not many people would be there at that time of day. But, Jesus met her at the well and asked for her to pour Him a drink.

As it was not appropriate for Jews to associate with Samaritans, she questioned this request, only for Him to respond:

"If you knew the gift of God and who it is that asks you for a drink, you would have asked him and he would have given you living water." —John chapter 4 verse 10

Jesus goes on to explain in verses 13-14: *"Everyone who drinks this water will be thirsty again, but whoever drinks the water I give them will never thirst. Indeed, the water I give them will become in them a spring of water welling up to eternal life."*

This woman's life was changed from that moment on. It doesn't matter who we are or what we've done, this living water that Jesus offers is for everyone who will drink from it.

Sometimes Jesus can be standing right in front of us offering springs of living water and we don't realise it. We keep going in our own strength, becoming weary until we stop midway in our path, but all along Jesus was asking us to stop and let Him give us rest and an abundant supply of living water *"welling up to eternal life"* (verse14).

"Come to me, all you who are weary and burdened, and I will give you rest." —Matthew chapter 11 verse 28

While it was awkward running out of fuel during a u-turn, it could have been a lot worse. I can be thankful that I didn't make it far enough to the motorway where the recommended speed is 100kmh. This could have been disastrous! God is always looking out for us and sometimes stopping us in our tracks is exactly what we need.

GOOD SAMARITANS

*I*t seems regardless of how prepared we think we are, we sometimes aren't prepared at all for what is to come.

A while ago, I embarked on a one day trip to Melbourne for an editing conference. I needed to jam-pack a lot into one day, so my alarm was set the day before and I'd packed everything I needed to take with me.

It started well. The 4.30am alarm buzzed, but I'd beaten the alarm and woken of my own accord. It seemed my mind was set on not missing that plane. The drive to my closest capital city airport was long, and far too early in the morning, but I made it, all in good time.

I caught the shuttle bus from my airport parking with perfect timing to allow myself plenty of space to check in and board my flight without breaking a sweat. That is, of course, until I broke something else.

I'll be fine!
Stepping out of the shuttle bus on my arrival at the airport, I slipped, and somehow whacked my toe repeatedly on the concrete gutter. Though shards of

pain shot through my foot, I gathered myself as best as I could and continued on my way, throwing an *I'm fine* smile to an onlooker to alleviate her look of concern.

Within a few steps, my foot began to throb and my toe swelled within my shoe. *I'll be fine!* I told myself again, knowing I had a big day ahead of me. *It's just bruised, I'm sure.*

Within minutes, I had broken into a pretty definite limp and was searching my bag for painkillers. Once on the plane, I managed to slip off my shoe and allow the swelling to have its way. Getting that shoe back on, however, was another issue.

Despite the pain, I managed to limp through the day with the help of an ice pack and painkillers and then turn around at the end of the day to get myself back home. The Melbourne airport is a big place, and I had never realised how big it was until I found myself at the opposite end that I was supposed to be.

Now with only 15 minutes until I needed to be on that plane, I limped and winced from one end of the airport to the other. Never had plane seating felt so good. But, by the time I got back to Brisbane that night, I was not feeling my best.

Putting on a brave face as I exited the plane, I couldn't help but notice the attendants looking at me a little strangely. Maybe the pain was evident in my facial expression or maybe it was my limp? Oh well. I continued on my way, not thinking too much about it, as all my efforts went into controlling my tolerance of my sore toe.

Me, the crazy lady
By this time, the pain caused me to make a few stops at chairs on my walk through the airport. At one such stop, a lady looked at me with an expression filled with pity. She started to walk towards me but her husband pulled her back as if to say, *Don't go there, she looks like a crazy lady!*

Instead, she mouthed the words to me, "Are you alright?" To which I smiled and said, "Yes, I'll be fine, I think I've just broken my toe. Thank you for asking."

I thought her husband's reaction was strange. It made me wonder how crazy I actually looked, so I limped to the closest bathroom.

When I saw my reflection in the mirror, I could understand the reactions I was receiving – I literally scared myself! It seemed that when I took the headphones off my head at the end of my flight my hair had blown right out of place and was standing upright in the air. Of course people were horrified! I was horrified! I truly looked like a limping, crazy lady with messy hair.

The visit to the doctor two days later confirmed my painful toe was not just broken, but broken in two places. I had good reason, after all, to be feeling so much pain. But, through it all, it was the thoughtfulness of that one lady that stood out to me.

Thinking beyond ourselves
Of all the people I passed in the busy airport terminals, one lady stopped to see if I was okay. Was that something I expected? Not necessarily. People are busy in their own worlds, just as I was. But this one woman reminded me of a good Samaritan.

To know that someone had noticed that I might have not been in the best situation, and acted on it, really was special in this day and age. It got me thinking – do I stop long enough to notice and to ask those around me, "Are you alright?"

It was nice that someone cared. It was nice that someone asked. It was simple, but it meant a lot.

"Which of these three do you think was a neighbour to the man who fell into the hands of robbers?" The expert in the law replied, "The one who had mercy on him." Jesus told him, "Go and do likewise." —Luke chapter 10 verses 36-37

Poem

THE TRAVELLER

Down amongst the hidden weathered chestnuts,
The traveller sat beside the open sea,
He pondered on the way that lay before him,
And gathered wandering thoughts he still believed.

The waves crashed in around the caverns,
The open caves disguised within the rocks,
The traveller watched the water thunderous rush them,
then quickly leave as if the ocean mocked.

The roughness of the sea disturbed him greatly,
He gathered up his things and trod alone,
Onto the country landscape stretched before him,
His thoughts were ones of want to lead him home.

And as the fields of wildflowers passed before him,
The solitude he longed for all around,
His laden heart felt heavy deep within him,
The earth was quiet, though his mind was loud.

"Where can I find the solitude I long for?"
Was heard in just a whisper from his mouth,
The whisper had a note of trialled anguish,
His heart was heard,
He travelled further south.

Weary now, he stopped to take a moment,
The waning light was lifting from his back,
The knotted log provided little comfort,
His pillow nothing better than his pack.

He watched the birds find shelter in their branches,
He watched the setting colours re-appear,
He heard the constant trickle of a fountain,
A song that sang so sweetly in his ear.

A whisper carried on the evening breezes,
A subtleness yet one could not ignore,
The gentleness of peace that soothes, releases,
The wonder of the words that heal it all.

"Come to me, oh treasured weary traveller,
Come to the fountain, I will give you rest.
Drink from the flowing water that is living,
And I will lift the burden from your chest."

And in that moment something deep within him,
Shouted from the hollowness inside,
"I want that living water that you speak of,
I want to leave my troubled heart behind!"

PIZZA AND CHOIR

The wonders of eternity embraced him,
He felt his life rejuvenate again,
The home he sought began to live within him,
And never did he walk alone again.

LIFESTYLE APP THAT DOES EVERYTHING IF ONLY!

For busy mums, it seems there are plenty of things that keep us on the go.

Besides housework, extra-curricular activities, never empty washing baskets, appointments, meals, shopping, and careers, the act of catching up with friends, family and celebrating special events is also important.

It's what I like to call *life in all its beauty* – it is busy, but it's good-busy. We are alive, so why not enjoy life's activities in all their colours?

These days, technology is growing in the number of ways it can apparently 'assist us' in order to make life easier and more organised. There are now a number of apps to help the busy mum such as: calendars where we can record our schedule with reminders; apps to help us budget and make shopping lists; apps to record our children's milestones, artwork, extra-curricular activities and even organise their share of chores for the week.

While these are all good and helpful, I often dream of apps that could do more. I am still looking for the app that will make the family meal for me after a long day of work; that will clean my house and pull the weeds from my garden.

Perhaps even one that will do my washing so that I can spend more time writing books, playing music, having fun, and spending time with my family with a never ceasing flow of energy for each activity.

Keeping up
It's a dream, I know, but one that I dare speak of at a time when I'm feeling fairly drained. I don't know about you, but sometimes my mind is more energetic than my body.

In a perfect world, we could run at full capacity at all times. But in this world, we do need to stop and be refreshed. At the end of the day, if we're not looking after ourselves, then we're no good to anyone else. It's all fun and games until your body has had enough.

A good friend recently observed my weariness and said to me, "You need to remember to take a drink from the river that flows from the Throne."

When I recalled the verses I had previously been reading, I realised that God was saying the same thing to me and I needed to stop a bit longer and really soak those words in:

"Be still and know that I am God," —Psalm chapter 46 verse 10

"Come all of you who are thirsty, come to the waters," —Isaiah chapter 55 verse 1

And my favourite:

"There is a river whose streams make glad the city of God, the holy place where the Most High dwells. God is within her, she will not fall; God will help her at break of day," —Psalm chapter 46 verses 4-5

Martha or Mary?
Sometimes it's easier to be a Martha than a Mary. If you're not familiar with the story in Luke's Gospel, Jesus visited the home of two sisters, Martha and Mary. While Martha busied herself preparing a meal, Mary sat at the feet of Jesus and listened to His words.

When Martha became annoyed with Mary's lack of activity, Jesus said, *"Martha, Martha, you are worried and upset about many things, but few things are needed - or indeed only one. Mary has chosen what is better, and it will not be taken away from her."* (paraphrased from Luke chapter 10 verses 38-41)

Mary had taken the time that was needed to listen and be refreshed by Jesus.

So, I'll let you in on a little secret, the refresh button at the top of the computer screen will not refresh you, nor will deleting all your emails or ticking your to-do boxes.

You actually need to stop, take time out and drink from the river that turns the dead to life – a river that truly refreshes and restores. The flowing river of God.

"Then the Angel showed me the river of the water of life, as clear as crystal, flowing from the throne of God and of the Lamb down the middle of the great street of the city. On each side of the river stood the tree of life, bearing twelve crops of fruit, yielding its fruit every month. And the leaves of the tree are for the healing of the nations." —Revelation chapter 22 verses 1-2

SPIDERMAN OR NOT?

My husband is a very intelligent and capable man – but when it comes to spiders, that's another thing altogether and intelligence swiftly succumbs to emotion.

Many years ago, when we were dating, we were driving to the wedding of some good friends of ours. I was working towards sitting for my driver's licence, so I decided to take the opportunity for some more driving practice and took the wheel that night. I was fairly calm and relaxed – until a massive huntsman spider began climbing across my windscreen!

Just keep driving
I don't know about you, but spiders are not exactly what I want to see on my windscreen while driving! We were on a road where it was not easy to pull over. I gasped and yelled, "What do I do?"

As scared as I was, there was still hope as the spider was on the outside of the screen where it could do me no harm. But, very quickly, it became apparent that the spider was on the inside of the window and just in front of my hands.

While my heart was beating at a hundred miles an hour, thankfully my husband was calm and instructed me not to worry.

"Just keep driving," he said sounding completely in control. "It won't get you."

Not wanting to look like an idiot, I listened to his steady instructions and managed to keep calm.

Wow, I thought, *he's so brave!*

"You're doing well, Beck," my husband reassured me. "He's not going to get you."

Next minute, the spider up and crawled across the windscreen to the passenger side. My husband leapt in his seat (seatbelt and all), yelling, "Pull over! Pull over!"

It's different when it's happening to you
After an attempt to use humour to calm him down by using his own words back on him – "He's not going to get you!" – I relented and pulled the car to the side of the road.

Sometimes life catches us by surprise. What is meant to be a fairly normal 'car ride' can suddenly become a challenge unprecedented from something totally unexpected being thrown into the mix.

Some people refer to it as 'life throwing you a curve ball' or as 'throwing a spanner in the works'. Whatever it is called, it happens to all of us, and sometimes we just have to roll with the punches.

Though now we may call the spider episode amusing, often life's curveballs are not humorous – they are downright serious and painful.

While we may not know why and how trials suddenly fall upon us, maybe it is not for us to know or understand straight away. Often, we have to go through the trial before we see the outcome and understand the reason behind it.

We live in a world that is affected by sin – and in this world, a lot of bad stuff happens. However, many of us still know that God is loving and is constantly with us. We believe, and experience, that when we trust in God we find that His plan and purpose can overcome our trials.

These tough times can be part of our refining as people, just as for gold to be revealed, the soil has to be refined. Sometimes we can be so wrapped up in our trial that we forget to think of the ones who are going through it with us. But, that is when our eyes can be lifted, allowing us to help those beside us and perhaps make the load a little lighter as we carry each others burdens together.

Next time we're faced with something unexpected, I pray we will pause and put our mind on the Creator, asking, "What can I learn from this experience, God? How can I grow through this? How can I find your goodness here?" and, perhaps just as importantly, "How can I help others through this?"

HOLD THAT BOAT!

Standing in line quite a few years ago now, to board our very first cruise, my husband and I were filled with excitement.

This holiday couldn't have come at a better time. We were exhausted and fatigued and, with one week before we moved house, it was going to be the week of relaxation we so desperately needed.

How lovely it was that my in-laws could look after the children while we celebrated our wedding anniversary, and how nice it was going to be to have no cooking or cleaning to do. Yes, I was excited – this was to be the holiday I had dreamed of!

That was, of course, until we decided to use our time waiting in line to prepare the paperwork. I reached into the backpack and pulled out the passport covers. Much to our horror and disbelief, only one passport was inside!

"That's weird!" I said. We'd even stopped the car not long after we had left the house to double check we had the passports.

It turned out that it was the passport cases we'd seen, and not the actual passport!

But wait—it gets worse
Now, the predicament was to get worse. Not only were we in line for a cruise that was to leave in only two hours, but our house was one hour's drive away! So, working out the math ... we had exactly one hour for someone to drive to our house and – if they were lucky enough to even find the passport – one hour for them to drive back in time for us to board the ship. That was not going to be easy.

It was, however, our only hope. We made a call to my in-laws, who had positioned themselves with our children beside the river to wave us off when the ship left. Thankfully, they were up for the challenge. While my mother-in-law drove to their house nearby to see if we'd left the passport there, my father-in-law took our car and began the drive to our house an hour away to see if the passport was there. At least we couldn't say we didn't try!

When all else fails ...
We stood in line, unable to do anything but wait ...and panic! Then the phone rang.

"We had to stop for petrol!"

Aaah! This was getting worse by the minute. Of course, we hadn't worried about putting more petrol in the car as we were going to be away. The clock was ticking and we were losing valuable minutes.

While we waited, we watched the other passengers finalise their paperwork and board the ship, and observed the staff pack down all the chairs and tables, leaving the room looking, once again, like an empty warehouse.

We stood at the edge of the dock with one of the ship's officers and the last remaining staff who were hoping as much as we were that the passport would arrive in time – but it was not looking good. Our bags had been removed from the ship and sat next to us. Tears were shed as I began imagining my week not on that boat.

Working for our good
However, while we waited, things were working for our good. Even when all things seemed to be going against us, the energy and determination of those we loved were working overtime *for* us.

"We really have only two minutes before we have to board," the officer said, "but I'll stay until the last possible second."

With less than a minute to go, the ropes were being released and the gang plank prepared for final removal. We could hear the engines revving in anticipation of the pull-away as the Captain's second in-charge stood beside us looking at her watch as they tried to give us every last possible second.

It was at that moment my son's silhouette appeared in the distant doorway calling, "Dad! We've got it!"

My husband ran like never before to meet him, and without even a second for an embrace, the exchange was made and my husband was running back towards the ship. Like a scene in a movie, we leapt onto the ship in one swift movement holding our bags, the door shutting behind us as the ship left the dock.

Recovery
Needless to say, it took us three days to recover from that incident, but thankfully we were on a holiday well suited for recovery. On the final evening of the cruise, we were invited to have dinner with the captain of the ship. When we told him our story, his response (after a good belly-shaking chuckle) was, "Oh! So you're *that* couple!"

Unfortunately, we were *that* couple. But I can safely say, we learnt our lesson, and never again have we, nor anyone who has heard our story, ever forgotten their passport again.

Now for the biblical relevance
Have you ever noticed that when things seem really bad, there comes a point where the bad is met with equal good that has the power to overcome it? It's like how climbing to the precipice of a mountain, with that painstaking effort to get there, ends up being so very much worth the journey. While our trial was intense, it was only for a short and momentary time.

Getting to that breakthrough, though, requires efforts and extraordinary measures – and things beyond our power.

In the midst of life's intense trials, as they seem to only escalate, at some point those extraordinary measures will see the bad encounter the good, leading something to break, and bad giving way to good. Strength rises to meet its adversary and in the process we realise how much we have grown with the experience.

It's not our own strength that we can brag about in the overcoming of these obstacles, instead these trials are used by God to grow our strength and our faith in Him.

The reality is, if we never wanted or needed for anything, there would be no reason for us to grow. We would simply stagnate, and everyone knows that when water stands stagnant for too long, it begins to smell.

I've often wondered why such things happen in the first place, but with some distance from the experience I can look back and realise that all things do work out for good for those who love the Lord.

While smooth-sailing sounds nice, it's the bumps in the road that make us stronger and brings us together.

"For this light momentary affliction is preparing for us an eternal weight of glory beyond all comparison, as we look not to the things that are seen but to the things that are unseen. For the things that are seen are transient, but the things that are unseen are eternal."
—2 Corinthians chapter 4 verses 17-18

AUTUMN

—The weather cools, the shadows become longer and the days become shorter. The cooling weather soothes like a salve on a sunburnt skin.

LET'S GET REAL MOTHER'S DAY MASH-UP

I didn't have many expectations for Mother's Day.

I generally like to enjoy however it comes, but I did have one pre-requisite – that there be no sibling arguing.

I say this with a grin: Mother's Day can be hard on the family. When mum has a day off it means that everyone else has to do the things mum normally does for themselves. Thankfully for them, it only happens once a year.

I knew it was going to be a busy Mother's Day this year, with commitments at church as well as family to pick up from the airport etc. So, when I was able to sleep-in the day before for the first time in months, I was very pleased ... and a little suspicious. *Is God giving me extra rest today for a reason?*

Sunday morning came and everything was going well – then not so well. A trigger from one child sent another one of my children off like a train, letting off steam with a passion! As I slipped out of the room and into the laundry to find a quiet space, I noticed that my washing machine was flashing 'F3' at me.

Investigation revealed it had come off its hinges due to a broken suspension and dirty washing was already piling up in the bucket. As you can imagine, that's not good news for a family of six.

Happy Mother's Day!
This beginning set the tone for the day and meant we didn't get the annual family photo. While there were lesser 'hallmark' moments for us, scrolling through social media over the course of the day and seeing the beautiful family Mother's Day photos of my friends, only reminded me that ours would not be one of them.

My well-meaning children scurried to pull together whatever was left of the day and it began to improve, but my request for no arguing had long since gone out the window.

You had one job
While not everything in life is meant to be easy, I was hopeful that the one day of the year meant to be my day off would be just that. Instead, it ended up requiring more mothering skills and calmness from me than usual, leaving me fighting off the temptation to feel sorry for myself.

But, though the day wasn't perfect, it was real. Families are not always picture perfect, they are not always "insta-worthy", and special days don't always run as planned. Families are however, a gathering of different personalities that often complement each other, but can also clash. It can be messy, it can be loud – but it can also be so much fun.

What's wonderful is that families are all in it together and despite their differences, whether it be a clash of wills, stubbornness or tiredness, the love doesn't have to change. It just needs to bear with each other.

My children know that in this house they are safe, that they belong, and that they are loved even with their imperfections – because we are aware that we all have them.

They know that even when we fail or make mistakes, it doesn't affect our love for each other – though a little gentle shaping may be in order.

We are safe, we belong, and we are loved
Often, we don't measure up to our own expectations and, though we may have the best intentions, sometimes we mess up. But, even when we feel like we've failed God, here in His love we are safe, we belong and we are loved – but we are also shaped.

Proverbs chapter 3 verse 12 says: *'... the Lord disciplines those he loves, as a father the son he delights in.'*

When God gives us a nudge in the right direction, it can sometimes be uncomfortable, but it's because He loves us enough to show us how we can be better. He never rejects us – even in our imperfections He still lavishes His love upon us.

'Therefore, as God's chosen people, holy and dearly loved, clothe yourselves with compassion, kindness, humility, gentleness and patience. Bear with each other and forgive one another if any of you has a grievance against someone. Forgive as the Lord forgave you. And over all these virtues put on love, which binds them all together in perfect unity. Let the peace of Christ rule in your hearts, since as members of one body you were called to peace. And be thankful.' —Colossians chapter 3 verses 12-15

For all the mums out there who spend Mother's Day looking for a silver lining, I just want to say thank you for loving your family through the glorious days and the not-so-glorious days. And, hey … there's always next year!

THAT WAS NOT MY INTENTION

ometimes I can't help but giggle a little on the inside.

This usually happens when somebody says something like: "Oh, your kids are so well behaved." At that moment, my mind will wander to so many things, one of which is a special moment many years ago when my two eldest children were around the ages of two and three.

We called them "creative toddlers". It was the only way we could see any purpose in the antics they used to get up to together. One particular morning, my husband and I awoke to the smell of smoke.

We'd learned the necessity of the many child locks and gates we had put on doors, fridges and cupboards, but these children were brilliant and outdid anything the experts in the child safety industry could come up with to keep them safe.

As I rose quickly to investigate where the burning smell was coming from, I found myself speechless. I literally didn't know how to put the scene that lay before me into words. Only now, many years later, I can.

Still waking up after only four hours sleep, I found my two little cherubs sitting at their child size table in the lounge area, with huge smiles on their faces. While that might sound nice, I couldn't see the table they were sitting at due to the layers of glistening oats and honey spread across it – and onto the floor!

Next, my eyes were drawn to the kitchen bench which reflected a similar scene of oats, milk and empty cordial bottles. Empty cordial bottles? Following the mess to kitchen, I quickly realised where the cordial was when my feet splashed through sticky liquid flooding my kitchen floor.

Realising the burnt smell was coming from the microwave, I opened it to find my basting brush frizzled to an unrecognisable shape sitting inside a bowl of … well, who really knows?

Unable to speak, I returned to my bedroom passing my two "cherubs" on the way. They were looking very proud of themselves, and boldly announced, "Look mummy! We made breakfast!"

All I could say to my husband was, "You need to take a look."

Our next course of action was to put the "cherubs" in the bathtub while we spent the next hour or so cleaning up after "breakfast".

I'd never actually been speechless before. It was an odd feeling and one I didn't really want to ever re-live quite like that again. But, there were to be more of these days.

For weeks afterwards, we suffered post-traumatic flashbacks, the sound of our feet sticking to the floor bringing back fresh memories of that eventful morning time and time again.

Although we did give the children a good talking to about not putting things in the microwave, I don't remember getting angry at my toddlers over this incident – probably because it took so long to recover from the shock of it.

While *we* saw this incident as a major mess and possible catastrophic kitchen incident, our children saw it as a gift to us. In their young minds, they were making us breakfast and were very proud of their efforts.

The motivation behind that morning's events was love, though I'm just grateful they didn't decide to give us breakfast in bed – but if I hadn't risen when I did, it probably would have been.

Sometimes people do things that immediately make us want to react negatively. But, what might appear to us as something hurtful, or that may harm us or cause us more work, might not always be what it first seems to be. Instead, it may just be an accidental outcome which first began with the intention of kindness.

When we are willing to pause for a moment, take some deep breaths, and look at the situation through someone else's eyes, we may be surprised at what we find. Who knows – we may discover that the intention behind the actions was born out of love, rather than a desire to harm.

REMOVING THE SPIRIT OF HEAVINESS

Some days, every car on the road seems to be in the way, phone calls are an interruption, all the voices around us seem to be complaining about one thing or another, and we have a mountain of work in front of us that we just can't seem to get to.

Feeling heavy? Most of us have days like this and sometimes all we can do is get everything into order so that something purposeful gets accomplished.

Pressing in on every side
In Luke chapter 8 verses 40-56, we read about a day when Jesus was on His way to heal the 12-year-old daughter of a synagogue leader. As He walked, He found Himself surrounded by people, so many that they were pressing in on every side, almost crushing Him.

For many people, these obstacles working against getting to this urgent destination on time would probably create a great deal of frustration and stress. But, Jesus knew there was a purpose in every step and He was not perturbed.

While He was making His way to the home of the sick girl, a woman who had been subject to bleeding for twelve years touched His cloak. What the disciples found strangest about it, though, was how Jesus responded – asking who touched Him.

There were countless people in the crowd pressing against Him as He walked, but it was this one touch amongst many that was a touch of faith. Hoping for a miracle, the woman who touched the hem of Jesus' cloak believed that He had the power to heal her – and her faith was rewarded. Jesus stopped, addressed her as 'daughter' and blessed her.

Daughters of the King arise
While all this was happening, the waiting synagogue leader, Jairus, received word that his daughter was dead and that he shouldn't bother the teacher anymore.

'Hearing this, Jesus said to Jairus, *"Don't be afraid; just believe, and she will be healed."* —Luke chapter 8 verse 50

Jesus had arrived at Jairus' house to find people were wailing and mourning because the girl had already died. But, He ignored the negative voices and made the way clear for a miracle.

'"Stop wailing," Jesus said. "She is not dead but asleep." They laughed at him, knowing that she was dead.' (verse 52-53)

When He entered the house, Jesus left the mourners outside, not letting any of them enter the room where Jairus' daughter lay. Instead, in a room where only those with faith and hope stood, He spoke to the little girl and told her to get up.

'Her spirit returned and at once she stood up.'
(verse 55)

Remove the complaining
Sometimes we need to remove the mourners from around us in order to accomplish that which God has called us to do. We need to relinquish the spirit of heaviness and replace it with the Spirit of the Lord, swapping it for the garment of praise. Praise changes the atmosphere and brings healing, comfort, liberty and beauty.

The Bible tells us that heaviness is a spirit (Isaiah chapter 61 verse 3) and we need to be rid of it. It is there only to cause distraction, obstacles and adversities which misdirect us from the path that God has mapped out for us.

When we feel nothing is going our way, that obstacles are clouding our view and getting in our way, that heaviness is weighing us down, that is the time to hand the heaviness over to God.

At the time, it can be a hard thing to push through as we feel that weight upon us. But, when we fill our hearts with praise and surround ourselves with people of faith, speaking truth, life and love, God is glorified and the things that come against us begin to disappear.

Jesus loves his daughters and sons, and there are no obstacles that can stop Him from reaching His destination of being with us. The question is – will we remove the obstacles of our making that prevent us from seeking Him?

"He has sent me…to comfort all who mourn, to console those who mourn in Zion, to give them beauty for ashes, the oil of joy for mourning, the garment of praise for the spirit of heaviness; that they may be called trees of righteousness, the planting of the Lord, that He may be glorified." —Isaiah chapter 61 verses 1-3

Poem

THE WINDS OF CHANGE

The winds of change swirl violently,
On my rooftop, battering,
Around the windows, frantically,
And through the doorknobs, rattling.

I shut them out emphatically,
They do not dare invade,
If I should just pretend they're gone,
Perhaps indeed they'll fade.

The winds of change intensify,
Gaining speed and fervour,
Within my quiet sanctuary,
I wish for sleep and nurture.

The safety of my walls do shake,
They crack and strain under the quake,
I huddle further from the storm,
My shelter is no longer warm.

REBECCA MOORE

"Be gone!" I call to it aloud,
"Do not, my comfort, overcrowd!
It's nice in here, that was until,
my sanctuary you now have filled!"

It broke in through a window clear,
and dashed what once was held so dear,
It shook the rafters, shook the floor,
until there was no wall at all!

It battered at the chimney standing,
Until it fell upon the landing,
It threw the tables all around,
Until the house came tumbling down.

"Now why did you my comfort take?
What is the cause of this mistake?
I had the walls just where they be,
They suited what I like, you see!"

Just then the wind tousled my hair,
the purpose to divert my stare,
For what I hadn't seen before,
Had once been blocked by one tall wall.

And then I turned another way,
and saw what only had been grey,
A garden lay beyond the fetter,
I like this landscape so much better.

PIZZA AND CHOIR

How could it be I did not know,
That here the daffodils could grow?
How could it be the colours bright,
Could open and invade my night?

I thought my little sanctuary,
was better than all else,
I thought the walls of dull grey ash,
Were all that could be felt.

And now the winds of change had ceased,
I watched them fly away,
To other lands they would bring peace,
But first a violent ray.

ROAD MAPS AND DETOURS

I typed the location into my maps app. I was on a road I knew well, and the street I was looking for wasn't far, but I had just never needed to find it before.

The good old maps app decided to take me on a detour. It wasn't the fastest possible route to my destination and as I came out of the unnecessary loop it took me on, I couldn't help but feel a little frustrated.

I could see that I would have saved some time if I'd just stayed on the road I was already on and, instead of taking a detour to the left, I could have just turned right at the next round about.

Thankfully, God's road map is accurate. But, sometimes we still feel like we've been taken on a detour and getting to our destination is taking much longer than we anticipated. We can see the outcome we would like, but we can't see the purpose of everything along the way.

Ever felt like that? Ever felt like if you could just take the reins, you'd get the job done faster?

A bigger plan

In Luke chapter 1, we read of Elizabeth's life-long desire for a child. Though it seemed to come easily for all the other women around her, it was something that just wasn't looking like it was ever going to happen for Elizabeth.

The emotional impact of not being able to have a baby may have been hard to understand for those who knew them. Zechariah and Elizabeth were righteous people who trusted in and pleased the Lord despite their life-long heartache. Elizabeth's father had been a priest and she'd also married one. Her family would have been highly esteemed in her community.

However, it didn't seem to matter how righteous this couple was. Bearing the burden of childlessness had taken such a toll on them that, when Zechariah was face to face with the archangel Gabriel, he was hesitant to believe that their prayer was about to be answered.

'Zechariah asked the angel, "How can I be sure of this? I am an old man and my wife is well along in years."
—Luke chapter 2 verse 18

The angel said to him, *"I am Gabriel. I stand in the presence of God, and I have been sent to speak to you and to tell you this good news. And now you will be silent and not able to speak until the day this happens, because you did not believe my words, which will come true at their appointed time."*

God is faithful
God had always planned for Zechariah and Elizabeth to bear a child, and their son was to be a very special child, with powers and influence not seen since the prophet Elijah. John was to be a prophet of the Most High, sent to prepare the way for the most important visitor the earth had ever received – Jesus Christ.

You see, God had a plan all along. If Elizabeth had borne children in her younger years, there would be nothing to make this child stand out as being different from the others. The miracle of this baby being born in Elizabeth's old age, was striking.

The timing was impeccable, occurring six months prior to his cousin Jesus being born. And, the outcome was astounding. Zechariah was released from his muteness right after announcing in the form of writing that his son would be called John.

'He asked for a writing tablet, and to everyone's astonishment he wrote, "His name is John." Immediately his mouth was opened and his tongue set free, and he began to speak, praising God. All the neighbours were filled with awe, and throughout the hill country of Judea people were talking about all these

things. Everyone who heard this wondered about it, asking, "What then is this child going to be?" For the Lord's hand was with him.'
—Luke chapter 1 verses 63-66

All these things coming together caused the people to stop and acknowledge that this was a fulfillment of God's purpose – that this child was set apart.

God's detours are blessings in disguise
God is not slow to keep his promises – His timing is perfect, right down to the last minute. We aren't the author of this book, but if we're willing and trusting we get to be a purposeful character in it.

So, if God wants to take us on what looks like a detour, we can know it's a very purposeful detour designed to deliver us to a perfect destination. And, when we arrive we will marvel at the power and the always perfect timing of our awesome God.

"Even Elizabeth your relative is going to have a child in her old age, and she who was said to be unable to conceive is in her sixth month. For no word from God will ever fail." —Luke chapter 1 verses 36-37

I COULD'VE KICKED MYSELF!

Have you ever heard the phrase, "I could've kicked myself!"?

It's a funny phrase, especially to visual people who can imagine what that would look like. It's usually used when one regrets something they've done e.g. "I could've kicked myself for not getting that when it was on special!" or "I could've kicked myself for saying that!"

It's actually really difficult to literally kick yourself, though. Reflexes set in and you stop yourself before you get hurt (not that I've tried it).

Regret is a painful thing
All that aside, what this phrase is really talking about is 'regret'. The Cambridge online dictionary defines regret as being *'a feeling of sadness about something sad or wrong or about a mistake that you have made, and a wish that it could have been different and better.'*

Often, we can say things that we wish we could take back. For instance, recently as I was taking some garlic bread my daughter had prepared from the oven, I joked about the multiple layers of foil wrapping saying, "Looks like they got the work-experience kid to wrap these!"

I'd assumed they had been pre-packaged, but I quickly realised I was mistaken when I saw my daughter's look of shock followed by, "Mum! I wrapped those!"

Thankfully, we just laughed at my careless words, but it's not always that easy. Sometimes what makes sense in our heads comes out of our mouths sounding very different.

Careless whispers
Often we can find ourselves regretting unintentionally causing pain to a friend, be it through careless words, actions or even lack of action. Though causing pain wasn't our intention, there's many a time miscommunications occur and our words can be taken the wrong way.

This is something most of us have been guilty of at some point, and we need to be alert to the fact that the enemy loves to use these opportunities to cause division.

It's very likely to be something that will happen many times in our lives. Inevitably, people will say things that might offend us, and we will say things that offend others whether we mean to or not. But, we can choose to be offended or we can choose to be forgiving – knowing that we ourselves have been guilty of the same.

Ecclesiastes chapter 7 verses 20-22 says: *'Indeed, there is no one on earth who is righteous, no one who does what is right and never sins. Do not pay attention to every word people say, or you may hear your servant cursing you — for you know in your heart that many times you yourself have cursed others.'*

Good regret
The good news is, that though we may mentally beat ourselves up over regret, it's not the end of the story. We may regret what we say and do, but God is quick to forgive and set us straight again.

As 2 Corinthians chapter 7 tells us that some sorrow is good for us: *'Godly sorrow brings repentance that leads to salvation and leaves no regret, but worldly sorrow brings death. See what this godly sorrow has produced in you: what earnestness, what eagerness to clear yourselves, what indignation, what alarm, what longing, what concern, what readiness to see justice done.'*

Sometimes regrets cause us to step up – step up in our character and to step up in our awareness. That's when the pain of regret can turn into something very beautiful. We are continually being transformed into the likeness of Jesus and, through our imperfections, His light and glory is seen brighter.

We are weak, but His grace is strong in us and, as we carry the forgiveness of Christ, we in turn learn to forgive others, for we know we are all sinners who have been saved.

Romans chapter 3 verse 22 says, *'This righteousness is given through faith in Jesus Christ to all who believe. There is no difference between Jew and Gentile, for all have sinned and fall short of the glory of God, and all are justified freely by his grace through the redemption that came by Christ Jesus.'*

Through each mistake, we grow more earnest in our desire to be better, to be more caring, and to be more thoughtful. And, we are renewed daily by the love of Christ.

'Because of the Lord's great love we are not consumed, for his compassions never fail. They are new every morning; great is your faithfulness.' —Lamentations chapter 3 verses 22-23

A WALK IN THE RAIN

When one of my daughters was around six years old, she really pushed the limits.

Her little tirade was over nothing memorable, yet she let the household know exactly how she felt.

Watching my husband's face as we stood aghast at her six-year old tantrum and wondering what he was going to do, I deliberated on whether to step in or let him deal with this.

My thoughts on how I'd deal with her were to discipline her and send her to her room. But, taking a deep breath, my husband looked her in the eye and said, "Let's go for a walk."

"I don't want to go for a walk!" she replied, stomping her little foot on the ground and crossing her arms in front of her.

"Let's go for a walk," he said again, and took her hand.

Hesitantly, she trudged out the front door with him, her brow creased with cranky lines and her little mouth tightly pursed. She was adamant she was not going to enjoy this.

As they left, I prayed. I prayed that my daughter would calm down and that my husband would know the right words to say.

It was lightly raining when they left, just a gentle shower, enough to sprinkle on their heads but not enough to soak them. Hopefully, it would just add to the adventure of the walk.

But, as time ticked by, the light shower quickly turned into torrential bucketing rain – and they were still out! I was worried for them, and worried that our little miss might come home more miserable than when she left.

They were out for a while longer, but when they returned I was surprised and delighted to hear the sound of laughter and to see big smiles on their faces, and excited stories coming from the lips of my previously cranky daughter.

"What happened?" I asked, pleasantly bewildered. "What did you say to her?" (This guy had some serious parenting skills that I was keen to get hold of!)

"Nothing," he replied. Thinking he was just being modest, I probed him for more information.

"You must have said something?"

He explained that he really didn't say anything. They had walked in silence most of the way and then it rained. The rain was heavy, so they took shelter under a tree. It had fruit on it, which they picked while getting completely drenched by the rain.

With the breaking of the clouds came the breaking of the mood. Our little girl had needed time out, and just being with her daddy was all that was needed for her to see perspective once again.

Sometimes we all just need to be with our daddy – that is, our Heavenly Dad. The late nights may be piling up, things may be annoying us, and there is no real reason to be out-of-sorts – we just are. That's when we need to be still the most.

Psalm chapter 46 verse 10 says: *"Be still, and know that I am God"*.

When we are still, we rest, we listen, and we are refreshed. Finding the quiet can be hard to do in this busy world of ours, but when those spaces are found, we see how necessary they are for us to focus again on what's important, to get our eyes off our problems and gain a fresh new view of the world through the eyes of the One who holds the world in His hands.

In the New Testament, we see Jesus Himself showing us an example of finding those spaces and spending time with his Father to refresh:

'But now even more the report about him went abroad, and great crowds gathered to hear him and to be healed of their infirmities. But he would withdraw to desolate places and pray.' —Luke chapter 5 verses 15-16

If it was important for Jesus to spend time with the Father, then how much more important is it for us? Closing our eyes and soaking in His presence not only calms our mind, but refreshes our souls – we don't even need to say anything.

Next time you're feeling a little stressed out, maybe 'take a walk in the rain' with your Heavenly Father. Let Him know how you're feeling and just be still.

'Take my yoke upon you, and learn from me, for I am gentle and lowly in heart: and you will find rest for your souls.' —Matthew chapter 11 verse 29

WINTER

—we make the most of wearing jackets and jumpers, huddled up around a bonfire where marshmallows toast until almost burnt. We explore the frosty hinterland, while still able to enjoy sunny walks along the beach.

THE GOD OF THE HILLS AND VALLEYS

Last night I dreamed about a time when my children were babies. I was back in the house we used to live in, reliving a day in my life from years earlier.

Everything looked and smelt the same – the colour of the walls, my kitchen where I prepared countless meals, the scent of the jasmine flowing through the window, and my baby's sweet smiles and chubby little faces.

It was a beautiful dream, up until the new owners of our old house came home. The moment turned awkward as I found I was trespassing in someone else's home.

As the reality dawned upon me that this joyful era had passed, I sobbed in my dream, realising that my babies had grown up and that time had moved on.

Can't go back
My sadness was not so much about our old house. I love where we live now, though the memories we created in that home are precious and hold a very dear place in my heart.

No, my sadness had more to do with the fact that this moment in time with my babies had passed, and the knowledge that I couldn't go back and visit them at that age again tugged at my heart.

These days, I can't pick their little bodies up and carry them in my arms or give them piggy-back rides – if I tried that now, it might cause an injury!

God knows how sentimental us mothers get and, though we may sometimes feel silly for feeling emotional over seemingly small things, those feelings come from great love and are precious to our Father God.

Psalm chapter 56 verse 8 says: *'You number my wanderings; put my tears into your bottle; are they not in Your book?'*

I am not alone
I realise the journey we have been on since the baby days has been full of mountains and valleys, joys and challenges, victories and heartache. Though God has not taken the hard things away from us, He has certainly walked with us as we went through them.

I don't know about you, but sometimes my dreams have their own soundtrack or theme song. The song that was playing through my mind in this dream seemed a perfect fit:

PIZZA AND CHOIR

I've walked among the shadows
You wiped my tears away
And I've felt the pain of heartbreak
And I've seen the brighter days
And I've prayed prayers to heaven from my
lowest place
And I have held the blessings
God, you give and take away

On the mountains, I will bow my life
To the one who set me there
In the valley, I will lift my eyes to the one
who sees me there
when I'm standing on the mountain aft,
didn't get there on my own
When I'm walking through the valley end,
no I am not alone!
You're the God of the hills and valleys
And I am not alone.

(Hills and Valleys by Tauren Wells—co-written with Chuck Butler and Jonathan Smith)

Close to His heart

After waking from that dream, I pondered on the years that have passed since then. I know full well that every stage of my children's lives is just as precious as those baby days and I'm grateful for each and every moment.

I'm also grateful that we don't have to parent alone. Isaiah chapter 40 verse 11 says: *'He tends his flock like a shepherd: He gathers the lambs in his arms and carries them close to his heart; he gently leads those that have young.'*

Children are a gift from God and every moment is precious. As my children reach for their own dreams in life, I can take assurance in the knowledge that my Father in Heaven is their Father too. When I can't be there with them, I know there is One who is always by their side – and I can take comfort in that.

'In peace I will lie down and sleep, for you alone, Lord, make me dwell in safety.'—Psalm chapter 4 verse 8.

Poem

THEY MET IN THE PARK WITH THE LEAVES

Swept up in the breeze,
    were the course brown leaves,
        swept up in the twist of the air.

A sharp swirl and a toss,
and a tear at the loss,
brown leaves tumbled down on her hair.

Just one look at the dross,
of the leaves and the moss,
As the tellings of age was compared.

Her eyes softened and played,
as an old leaf did lay,
Tawny red in the cup of her hand.

She lifted it high,
To dance with the sky,
She lifted it high in the air.

REBECCA MOORE

"We shall dance to the music,
of times long ago,
we shall dance to the days now so rare."

Held close in her hand,
he did understand,
that his tree was now far far away.

Long gone was the brush,
of the foliage so green,
Long gone was the tree's golden ray.

How he longed for the days,
he provided the shade,
for the children who played underneath.

The branches that held,
onto leaves just like him,
The branches that sheltered from heat.

Now he danced in the breeze,
held with great ease,
by a child, young and so full of life.

And he tossed and he twirled,
And he saw the whole world,
then the day quickly turned into night.

PIZZA AND CHOIR

The girl looked at the leaf,
and feeling his grief,
she turned to her mother and said,

"I shall frame him!" she cried
"then he's always alive,"
and homewards her mother then led.

For this day they both shared,
escape from their cares,
for a moment they both felt some ease.

Then he sat on her wall,
never more would he fall,
never more would he float on the breeze.

And she played underneath,
well out of the heat,
and the breeze and the shade of the trees.

But the moment they shared,
would always be there,
how they met in the park with the leaves.

NOT FINISHED YET

After the passing of Rev. Billy Graham, I found myself thinking about what it means to age in Christ.

Here we had a beautiful godly man who was used by God to bless others right up until the day of his passing into the presence of his Lord.

Billy Graham's life offers all of us a great example of what a 'good and faithful servant' looks like, and shows a man who looked forward to entering heaven's gates with great anticipation.

This quote sums up well what heaven meant to him:

"Someday you will read or hear that Billy Graham is dead. Don't you believe a word of it. I shall be more alive than I am now. I will just have changed my address. I will have gone into the presence of God."
—Billy Graham

Until our time on earth is done
There is something truly wonderful about the way in which God has given us all special gifts. Some people, however, feel that once they reach a certain age, their gifts are no longer valuable or useful.

It is sad, but true, that this is a common thought process amongst the ageing. Whether it comes from the way they are treated by others, or from their own thought conversations, growing older can make many feel 'out of the game' or like 'the ship has sailed'.

It is said that there comes a moment in life where many people feel they have become 'invisible' – a sense of no longer being useful or even noticed – most commonly due to age. We live in a world that predominantly focusses on younger generations, yet there is so much to be learnt from all ages with a broad spectrum of beauty to be captured.

Don't let anyone look down on you
– even if you're old
We often hear the Scripture passage quoted from 1 Timothy chapter 4 verse 12 that says:

"Don't let anyone look down on you because you are young, but set an example for the believers in speech, in conduct, in love, in faith and in purity."

This is a wonderful verse, showing us that God is keen for us to get started in Kingdom work asap.

On the other end of the scale, we are also commanded to honour those who are older. This verse is not quoted as often as the first verse, but balances it out beautifully:

"The elders who direct the affairs of the church well are worthy of double honour, especially those whose work is preaching and teaching. For Scripture says, "Do not muzzle an ox while it is treading out the grain," and "The worker deserves his wages."'
—1 Timothy chapter 5 verses 17-18

Treading out the grain

While we are all growing older – even if we are young we are constantly getting older – it is good to remember that those *'good and faithful servants'*, whose focus is on God's work, are still continuously *'treading out the grain'*. This shouldn't cease simply because of the age divide or the appearance of grey hairs.

The elders in our midst are a kaleidoscope of colours drawn from years of 'life'. If we could imagine each year lived as a texture or a colour on a 'coat of life', imagine the magnificent coats our 'mature friends' are wearing!

Each have a set of experiences unique to them, growing in the wisdom and understanding that only age and experience can bring with each passing year. They are a treasure trove of wonderful insights and are worthy of the time it takes to pause, learn and soak in their knowledge.

Never too old
I was recently speaking with a lovely 'mature-aged' woman at a church function. I listened as she told me her story. She'd had a full life working in ministry and churches, until she was diagnosed with terminal cancer.

Praise be to God, she was miraculously and completely healed and, though she felt she was now too old to be of any use, God had other plans.

This child of God had been given a second chance in her mature years, a clear sign that God was not finished with her.

Her life is now heading in a new direction with fresh beginnings and opportunities opening up for her that are perfectly suited to her unique skill set.

God knew there was a specific need for her skills in the church. And, neither she nor anyone around her can know yet of the myriads of other ways God is going to use her to bless others along the way.

Not finished

The body of Christ is a beautiful thing, and not one part is useless. It doesn't matter how old we get, if we are still on this earth we haven't finished fulfilling God's purpose for us.

As we take the time to get to know each other, seeing God's expression through one another, may we love like we have been loved and bless as we have been blessed until the day we *"change our address"* and move *"into the presence of God"*.

"I thank my God every time I remember you. In all my prayers for all of you, I always pray with joy because of your partnership in the gospel from the first day until now, being confident of this, that he who began a good work in you will carry it on to completion until the day of Christ Jesus." —Philippians chapter 1 verses 3-6

HOW TO GET OFF A SKI LIFT

It wasn't until I was actually sitting on the ski lift that I realised I would have to get off.

We were on our honeymoon in New Zealand, and it was my first time skiing. I had my gear on and had managed to plonk myself onto the lift – skis and all.

It carried me up the slopes without stopping and, as I dealt with my fear of heights I suddenly realised – this lift was not going to come to a stop to let me off. I would have to jump off this thing with these huge, bulky skis strapped to my feet!

Images filled my mind of spending the afternoon going around and around on the ski lift, while my husband enjoyed the slopes.

"What if I can't get off and I just keep going?" I asked him.

Tony began to give me very concise and clear instructions about how to exit the ski lift and not fall over. I listened very carefully as I didn't want to mess this up. Soon enough, the moment to jump approached and he counted me down and said, "Now!"

Nervously, I followed his instructions and successfully dismounted from the lift, smoothly gliding out of the way – all without falling over. To add to the skill required, it was snowing so much that day that we could barely see two metres in front of us. I was feeling very proud of myself for a couple of seconds, until I realised I could not see Tony.

I began calling his name. The snow was falling thickly and I assumed he was probably nearby and that I just couldn't see him through the blizzard. It was then I heard a faint and muffled call from what seemed a fair way away. It sounded like Tony, so I followed his voice and found him down an embankment.

"What are you doing down there?" I laughed. "I thought you knew how to do this?"

I was laughing so hard that I now couldn't see through my tears. It turned out he had never actually been on a ski lift either, and it had been a case of the blind leading the blind.

Sometimes that is how life feels. We are on a path, but the path in-front of us is not clear, it may even feel like it is clouded by a blizzard. And, when change is looming over us, it's comforting if we are able to know where it is taking us – but that is rarely the case.

To change the course of our path, sometimes we have to take a leap of faith. We can feel a pull in the right direction and, though what we are currently doing may be good, we know that feeling is temporary and courage is needed for the next step.

So, when the time comes, and God opens up a new path for us, we need to be ready to jump. It's exhilarating and frightening all at once.

Believing that God is for us and has a plan and purpose for our lives, we know that leaning on Him is the best way to be sure we're going to have a soft landing.

Sometimes, however, we like to do things in our own strength, and without seeking wisdom first. But, even when we make things harder than they need to be by our lack of trust and obedience, God uses these times to grow us, stretch us and mature us.

So, if you ever find yourself on one of life's ski lifts with no way to get off, listen very carefully to the instructions. You may find yourself gliding to the next ski field with ease, or maybe it will take some practise.

Either way, put your hope in God – He's got it all worked out and can see much further through the blizzards than we can.

Poem

FIERY CHARIOTS

Behind the wall, behind the door,
    Behind the whispers clear,
    My heart was still, my heart was full
        My heart, it did not fear.

For though the whispers brandished,
    The harshness and the lies,
    I knew the One who acted,
        On my heartfelt cries.

"Oh Father God, you know my heart,
    And though they misconstrue,
The words I try to speak to them,
    Will lead them to the truth.

"You're not alone, my precious one,
    I have prepared a way,
    And all these accusations,
    I will use to guide the day.

For though you do not see it now,
Your words will not fall short,
I speak them through your willing mouth,
They will not come to naught.

For there my children need to hear,
And some will come to know,
That everything I did till now,
My child, I did for those."

And through the painful whirlwind,
And through the hurtful cracks,
My Father held me strong and bold,
His strength withheld attacks.

And though it seemed I stood alone,
Surrounding me this night,
Were fiery chariots beyond count,
And angels filled with light.

LOOK OUT FOR THE BOWLING BALLS

*H*ave you ever had days, weeks or months when you have felt like you are a bowling pin at the end of a tenpin bowling lane?

As the bowling ball is aimed and released, you pray to God that ball is going to roll down the gutter. Sometimes the ball rolls and misses, other times it hits and, just as you get propped back up into position, along comes another one aimed directly your way.

Paul's bowling balls
When Paul was in Corinth teaching the Jews about Jesus, he had some pretty big bowling balls aimed his way. After receiving opposition and abuse from the Jewish leaders for some time, he'd eventually had enough, 'shook out his clothes' and moved on, taking his message to those who would appreciate it, which happened to be right next door.

Paul was still a little shaken up when the Lord appeared to him in a vision that very night saying: *"Do not be *afraid; keep on speaking, do not be silent for I am with you, and no one is going to attack and harm you, because I have many people in this city."*

So Paul stayed in Corinth for a year and a half, bringing the good news of Jesus to the Gentiles.

The Jews were still out of sorts with Paul and took him to the place of judgement, charging him with *'persuading the people to worship God in ways contrary to the law'*. But, before Paul could even open his mouth to defend himself, the proconsul Gallio basically told them he wasn't interested in listening to their petty charges about words and names and moved them on. God was truly looking after Paul. (paraphrased from Acts chapter 18)

False accusations
Paul faced a situation that is still common today: people accusing others of petty things, inventing stories to move people aside or pull others down – and all because they feel threatened. They assumed Paul was the enemy but, in actual fact, Paul was trying to save them from themselves.

Jesus dealt with even worse opposition and, just like Paul, He did not defend Himself. For Him, it was necessary to die for the purpose of the forgiveness of sins, and all the while, the ugliness of the human state was seen through these false accusations for what it was – ugly.

We've all probably been on both sides of this coin, both the accuser or the one being falsely accused. It's not pretty. May God forgive us for being the accuser, for even the Devil himself is the accuser of the saints (Revelation chapter 12 verse 10) – and God give us strength when we're the ones being accused.

Quick to assume without understanding
Unfortunately, people can often be quick to assume, and slow to look for the truth. But, as Jeremiah chapter 17 verse 10 says: *"I the Lord search the heart and examine the mind."*

Only God can fully know a person's heart. We cannot fully know another person's heart or true intentions, especially if we fail to take the time to seek understanding or genuinely enquire out of love for one another. Thankfully God knows His own, and allows us to learn and grow through these times.

His presence is always close, you just need to look for it. From simple things like the soothing sight of purple flowers growing and carpeting the ground surrounding jacaranda trees or the delicate fluttering of a myriad of migrating butterflies, from timely words from friends, to Bible verses jumping from the page and shields of peace amongst the arrows, God has His way of revealing Himself in the midst of seeming chaos.

We are not alone in our sufferings
There is always someone close by to help if we look – for Paul it was the house next door. When you feel unjustly criticised or are feeling the attacks one after another, it's often a good indicator that God is about to do something great. He is building your muscles of resilience, He is teaching you how to love the unlovely, He is teaching you how to lean on Him and trust.

Our initial reaction may be to rush in to defend ourselves or our loved ones, but God has a better plan if we can just lay low and trust Him.

Romans chapter 12 verses 19-20 says: *'Do not take revenge, my dear friends, but leave room for God's wrath, for it is written: "It is mine to avenge; I will repay," says the Lord. On the contrary: "If your enemy is hungry, feed him; if he is thirsty, give him something to drink. In doing this, you will heap burning coals on his head." Do not be overcome by evil, but overcome evil with good.'*

Stand
So, when you hear the pins reset and the rumble of the ball rolling down the bowling alley of life, allow your Father in Heaven to step in, and know that – even though it may get rough – He will help you to stand.

PIZZA AND CHOIR

'Therefore put on the full amor of God, so that when the day of evil comes, you may be able to stand your ground, and after you have done everything, to stand.'
—Ephesians chapter 6 verse 13

WORD-PLANTING

The seedling I'd planted looked nothing like the picture on the tag. It was gangly, small and looked like it might fall over at any moment, but the promise of the tag told me that this weak little plant would one day stand strong, with firm green leaves and grow a beautiful tall blue flower through the centre.

With excitement and expectation, I imagined how lovely this plant would one day look (as long as our pet goat didn't get to it first). I wedged the tag in the soil beside the seedling as a reminder of what it will one day become.

A few weeks on, having been nourished by good soil and bathed in regular rain showers and sunshine, the seedling had not fallen over but had gradually grown stronger. It will take time before it looks like the picture that sits beside it, but so long as it has good things going into it, I can be sure of its promise.

Big things come in little packages
I remember when my son was born. He seemed so little compared to my one and a half year old daughter, but I had a very strong feeling that one day this small baby

boy would grow to become a very tall and strong man. It took time, but my hunch was correct. A growth spurt at the age of 12 saw him suddenly shoot up, and today, now a young adult, that *little* boy of mine towers over us all.

When our children are small, we can spend much of our days wiping runny noses, changing nappies and cleaning messes. Those moments, though not always fun, are precious and important as they require love and caring.

While we may feel that what we're doing in those formative years is not very purposeful, those years are, in fact, some of the most foundational days of these little one's lives.

Early stages matter
A collaboration of seemingly insignificant things together makes for a strong foundation. These early days are also the times of story-telling, the times of song-singing, the times of play, and the first moments of word planting. Speaking words of encouragement, love and casting a vision of the wonderful person God has made them to be helps plant within our children a sense of purpose, love and belonging – not only to us, but to the One who created them.

Words such as: "You have such a beautiful heart"; "You, my boy are destined for greatness"; "I love how you do everything with such creativity"; "The way you play the drums, I can see you playing before kings and queens"; "When you dance, I love how it makes everyone smile".

It's not always at the forefront of our minds that one day these children are going to be adults, people who have influence and people who have been influenced. But, the words we plant in the beginning stages and along the way assist in growing healthy hearts, healthy minds and healthy bodies.

Seeing our children as future adults serves as a good reminder that we are not just managing children who will always be children, we are raising future leaders, husbands, wives, mothers, fathers, workers etc. The words we plant in them while they are small can largely affect how they see themselves as they grow – shaping and moulding them into the person they will become. Therefore, our words need to be loving, encouraging, empowering and pointing them in the right direction.

Speaking over us
Throughout the Bible, our Heavenly Father speaks over us. He sees us not just as we are, but as we will be. He spoke us into existence and continues speaking us into His predestined purpose for our lives.

'For he chose us in him before the creation of the world to be holy and blameless in his sight. In love he predestined us for adoption to sonship through Jesus Christ, in accordance with his pleasure and will—to the praise of his glorious grace, which he has freely given us in the One he loves.'
—Ephesians chapter 1 verses 4-6

And He continues to speak his words over us.

You are planned: *'Your eyes saw my unformed body; all the days ordained for me were written in your book before one of them came to be.'*
—Psalm chapter 139 verse 16

You are loved: *"I have loved you with an everlasting love; I have drawn you with unfailing kindness."*
—Jeremiah chapter 31 verse 3

You are fearfully and wonderfully made: *'I praise you because I am fearfully and wonderfully made.'*
—Psalm chapter 139 verse 14

You have a future and a hope: *'There is surely a future hope for you, and your hope will not be cut off.'*
—Proverbs chapter 23 verse 18

We all start from a small place but if we begin to see ourselves and others as God sees us, and shower ourselves with the watering can of promise and vision, we may begin to see the plant flourish, the stem and leaves growing strong, the petals taking shape, and the colours vibrantly glow – encouraging the other flowers of the garden to do the same.

SPRING

—brings a freshness and newness to the air. There is a floral fragrance to this season that reminds us that new life is imminent and Christmas is nearing. Not yet affected by the harshness of the Summer heat, Spring is a season of refreshment and energy, inviting us to play and marvel at the blossoming of nature.

YES MY DARLING, YOU WILL FLY

Many years ago, my-three-year-old ran frantically into the house after playing in the garden. She was beaming from ear to ear, grabbing our arms to pull us her way.

"Mummy! Daddy! Watch what I can do! It's so amazing!"

She pulled us through the back door and sat us down on the deck steps, making enough space between us for her to run through the middle. We were a little puzzled as she backed up against the door in order to get a run up, then she counted down fervently, "Three, two, one!" and took off running like Usain Bolt.

Still not quite sure what she was doing, I was shocked to see the amount of energy she was putting into her running as she followed the weaving brick pathway through the garden, and eventually to her swing. But, she didn't stop when she got to it.

With the speed she had built up from her run, she threw herself onto the swing, stomach first and arms stretched out like Superman. The swing caught her momentum and flew her up into the air!

"I'm flying!" she yelled.

The problem was, the swing stopped at some point in its arc to come down again, but our little girl kept going. Up, up, up, until gravity got the better of her little flight and she stopped in mid-air, falling to the ground with a thud.

Bewildered and amazed by the spectacle that had taken place before us, we picked our daughter up from the ground, dusting off her scuffed little knees and hands, and mending her wounds.

Apparently, it had gone much better when she was practicing it, but her dream of flying ended with a thud.

Lift off!
So often in life, we take off into our dreams filled with unbridled energy, confident that the path we're on will launch us into the atmosphere of untethered success – only to be met with a thud when reality gets the better of us.

What we thought was a clear path, we find is met with obstacles – obstacles that come in the form of many things, be it finance, closed doors, time restraints, or just needing someone who believes in our vision enough to share it. Sometimes, it could even be a lack of courage.

This, however, is not the end of the story. As much as the reality of our actions might have ended with a crash, still for a moment we were flying.

Each time we take action toward our purpose, God is there to cheer us as we fly, brush off our scuffed hands and knees if we fall, and stand us back up. He wants us to try again, and this time maybe do it a little differently – learning as we go. Each failure has something to teach us and as we learn, though the failures may hurt, can also make us stronger.

God knows the plans he has for us, and with each adversity, we'll be one step closer to the person He is shaping us to be, and to accomplishing the purpose He has placed in our hearts. We just have to find His path, and stick to it.

We can believe and know that our future successes are still before us and our path has not come to an end. It may have just taken a bend, but that bend in our path may lead us to a more beautiful road – and so we must walk on.

"In their hearts humans plan their course, but the Lord establishes their steps." —Proverbs chapter 16 verse 9

AWAITING BEAUTY

Anyone who knows me would know by the number of photos on my social media account that I like roses.

I have two rose plants that emit delicious fragrances, surpassing the fragrance of any Turkish Delight sweet I have come across. The only problem with my rose plants is that they all tend to flower around the same time as each other and then there are a few weeks where there is nothing.

During this time of no flowers, I find myself eagerly awaiting their beauty again. I spend time preparing for the flowering by tending the soil, watering, pruning and checking the leaves for bugs.

As the new shoots grow and begin to bud again, I find myself excited for the beauty that is promised in that little bud. I know the time is coming very soon when that bud will bloom again and I will be able to not only enjoy the beauty of the flower, but the fragrance that I have waited so long to smell.

Preparing the soil

It is often said that everyone is waiting for something, whether it be the promise of a child, a job, a house, or whatever it may be.

Ecclesiastes chapter three tells us there is a time for everything and a season for every activity under the heavens, the good and the bad. As we wait for the dreams and hopes to come about, our waiting is not in vain. Every step matters – and nothing goes to waste.

While we are waiting, and perhaps feel like we are in a season of toil, we are growing, and even the small things are being put to good use. They are feeding the soil to ready it for a healthy plant. Zechariah chapter 4 verse 10 says: *'Do not despise these small beginnings, for the Lord rejoices to see the work begin ...'*

It is in these small beginnings that God is planting the seed for something beautiful, and *'he who began a good work in you will carry it on to completion until the day of Jesus Christ,'* (Philippians chapter 1 verse 6). It is in the tending of the garden that the fruit is produced.

The bloom and the fragrance

Life is not meant to be easy, and sometimes the waiting on its own can be a marathon of endurance. But, we hold onto a hope that is greater than anything the world can offer. It exceeds the imaginations of our own plans and, though it may not bring fame and fortune, the miracles and the intricate weaving of the path God takes us on will leave us in awe and breathing in a fragrance above all others – the fragrance of Christ in our lives.

God is always at work, whether it is seen or unseen, and one day the waiting for beauty will flower and we will see that all the toil has been worth its while. And, if we're in a season of transformation between toil and harvest, then we can keep our hope – because one day we will bloom.

'How abundant are the good things that you have stored up for those who fear you ...'
—Psalm chapter 31 verse 19

Poem

THE GARDEN

My gaze rolled through the window to a garden,
To where my heart ran swift to catch the view,
It gently curled me up in sweet surrender,
Where all my cares and worries were subdued.

I wandered down the path that led to beauty,
Surrounded by the pink and purple hue,
A winding path that in itself was charming,
And all the coloured splendour was so new.

I came across an aged timber bench chair,
It welcomed me as if myself it knew,
I sat upon that aged timber bench chair,
Which swept me up, transporting me through blue.

The colours swirled and pirouetted round me,
The sky it seemed was more than just a haze,
It circled round, I felt as it embraced me,
I travelled a kaleidoscopic maze.

And though it seemed I sat alone on this chair,
I felt He sat beside me all the way,
His presence never leaving for one moment,
I did not fear, I knew that He would stay.

And then I saw He *was* the presence round me,
The colours and the beauty all so true,
He gathered all His loving powers round me,
And gently spoke,

"My small one … I love you."

"SQUARK!" IS NOT THE SOUND A CAR SHOULD MAKE

The sound of my grinding ignition could not be muffled – it was loud!

Each time I started up my little blue bomb of a car, it would give a screeching and a squeal, and I would pray to God that no one was nearby, (though that was seldom the case). Apparently, the technical term for the cause of the squawking was to do with a seized bearing in the starter motor thingy. Whatever it was called, it was not good.

Surrounded by prestige cars, there was no way of hiding my little blue bomb as I drove it out of the private-school car park each day. I would laugh it off as the other mothers glanced my way in horror at the sound which put everyone's teeth on edge, but secretly I was wishing I could disappear. I prayed for the day I could trade that thing in for a newer, nicer, quieter-starting model.

One day, I voiced my concern to my husband, explaining that the car was so embarrassing to drive, especially to the school, and it was surely about time to trade it in. His *helpful* advice at the time was, "Perhaps if you wash it and treat it as if it's your dream car, it might turn into something better."

My thoughts were, "If we want something better, maybe we should take it to the wrecker and purchase something else!"

Realising I was fighting an uphill battle, I decided I would do just what he suggested and see if my bomb would magically upgrade into something nicer. Each weekend, I ventured into my garage and began giving that neglected old car a good scrubbing. I had my little helpers, and together we scrubbed the roof, the bonnet and the boot, trying very hard to miss the rusted out holes in the corners and the edges.

We washed and polished the tyres and, as we did, a funny thing happened. The more I spent time making my bomb of a car look nice, the more I actually found myself feeling a little bit proud of it. Vacuuming the seats and shining up the paintwork, gave me a feeling of satisfaction and achievement, and even though it continued to squawk and carry-on at ignition, it didn't seem to bother me so much.

When the time finally came that the little blue bomb turned into a Volvo station wagon, I was well and truly ready to do the swap – but not without a little sentimental sadness (just a little). The car that had brought me embarrassment ended up teaching me that what seemed worthless could become something worthwhile by putting time and effort into it.

In Luke chapter 16, Jesus tells a parable about the Shrewd Manager who was about to lose his job, but made the most out of a bad situation by how he handled it and so was rewarded.

Jesus goes on to say in verses 10-12: *"Whoever can be trusted with very little can also be trusted with much, and whoever is dishonest with very little will also be dishonest with much. So if you have not been trustworthy in handling worldly wealth, who will trust you with true riches? And if you have not been trustworthy with someone else's property, who will give you property of your own?"*

When God gives us talents or gifts, we may not think we can do much with them. We may even think we are not worthy of them. But, even while we may be feeling like what we have and what we do is not worth much or is not effective or purposeful, often the opposite is true.

It is the small beginnings of things that set the foundation for what is to come. Whether it be in our jobs, our talents, or our relationships, if we take time to nurture and treat these areas with care, they may just blossom into something more beautiful than we ever imagined.

Now, I'm not saying that if we go out and wash our cars they will turn into a Ferrari (though my husband still lives in hope). It's not about the physical objects. It's all about attitudes, and by treating the seemingly insignificant areas of our lives with care, these areas then have room to grow. The training ground is often where it matters most.

"The hands of Zerubbabel have laid the foundation of this temple; his hands will also complete it. Then you will know that the Lord Almighty has sent me to you. Who dares despise the day of small things, since the seven eyes of the Lord that range throughout the earth will rejoice when they see the chosen capstone in the hand of Zerubbabel?" —Zechariah chapter 4 verses 9-10

SOCCER MUMS AND WELCOME DISTRACTIONS

I was a soccer mum for only a little while before we realised it probably wasn't our four year old's 'thing'. But, I distinctly remember finding the games to be endlessly amusing as I watched these little tots in their big shin pads and oversized uniforms scramble their way up and down the field trying to work out where they should be, whose team they were on, and where on earth did that ball go?

I'm sure there were parents though who did not share my amusement when we consistently lost – perhaps partly due to my son's distractions, social chatting and day-dreaming. What I thought was cute was probably really annoying to those who wanted to win.

Look out for the planes
One particular soccer match, the crowd of little four-year-olds ran in their cluster, with their eyes peeled to the ground as the ball went flying past their feet. Astounded that they didn't trip over each other while being so focussed and bunched on the field, I was puzzled when, all of a sudden, the entire group stopped to look to the sky.

The game came to a stand-still as the young players stood and stared in amazement at the plane flying overhead. Despite the encouragement of the coach and competitive parents on the side-line to keep going, nothing was going to happen until that plane had disappeared. And then, just like that, eyes were back to the field and realisation dawned on the pre-schoolers' faces as they recalled what they had been doing before the 'amazing plane' flew overhead.

Distractions - the good and the bad
Distractions are a fact of life. Some distractions are good, and some are not so good. Sometimes we get so focussed on our work and the serious things of life that a good distraction, such as a wedding or holiday trip, is just what we need to pull us out of our furrowed headspace and get us into a fresh frame of mind.

We can get so bogged down with distractions of 'must-do's' and time restraints that we forget to see the bigger picture of what actually matters. Sure, the game is important, but the wonder and awe those little children experienced in watching an enormous plane fly over them put both teams on the same level for a moment in time as they shared this astounding moment together.

The celestial eclipses normality
Living in such a highly contentious political time in history, some distractions are incredibly welcome. In

August of 2017, America witnessed what has been dubbed *The Great American Eclipse*. Proceeding the eclipse, an article was published in the Washington post entitled, *We are all just mind-boggled: Scenes from the total solar eclipse of 2017.*

In the 90 minutes it took for the country to witness this great phenomenon, all people, from lay workers to the President, were on one level as they stopped what they were doing to watch God's great power at work.

"On Monday, life in America was put on hold—the nagging to do list, the deadlines at work, the political debates and divisions. Everything receded, overtaken by the celestial event of the century suddenly looming over America."

Watching recorded highlights of the eclipse was a very emotional experience – even from the other side of the world!

Taking time out to remember how great our God is
While people cried, got tingles, and stood in awe, there were still another group who were uninterested, downplaying the wonder of the eclipse like it happens all the time.

People will call it what they want, but there's no denying God's greatness. While the earth is filled with

God's glory, we are still only seeing a glimpse of what is yet to come. There will be incredible, unspeakable wonders in eternity. Our earthly bodies just can't handle that kind of revelation and information yet.

1 Corinthians chapter 13 verse 12 says: *'For now we see only a reflection as in a mirror; then we shall see face to face. Now I know in part; then I shall know fully, even as I am fully known.'*

It is exciting when we think of the great God we serve

The Bible tells us of a man named Job who suffered incredible afflictions. After being mocked by his friends, who thought they knew him enough to make the accusation that his suffering had being brought on him due to hidden sin, the Lord speaks out of the storm posing questions about creation that didn't require an answer. Only God in His great and awesome power could have done such amazing things and knows the reasons for all the events that happen.

"Where were you when I laid the earth's foundation? Tell me, if you understand. Who marked off its dimensions? Surely you know! Who stretched a measuring line across it? On what were its footings set, or who laid its cornerstone—while the morning stars sang together and all the angels shouted for joy?"
—Job chapter 38 verses 4-7

In our human wisdom, we sometimes think we are so very smart. But who are we really? We should be honoured and humbled that a God who is so great would consider us children of His. This is where reverence and honour is birthed, when we realise our smallness is made great in His powerful love. We are unworthy, but God's great love shown through His Son, Jesus, makes us worthy.

'See what great love the Father has lavished on us, that we should be called children of God! And that is what we are! The reason the world does not know us is that it did not know him.' —1 John chapter 3 verse 1

So next time something wonderful happens, stop to absorb it, and lift your eyes heavenward – and thank God for the good distractions.

POEM – THE STAR THAT SAW THE WORLD

The darkness burst with brilliance,
   Lit by his fellow stars,
      Continued far beyond his view,
         'Twas beautiful and vast.

They stood there in their places,
   the debonair and strong,
   the planets lined the corridors,
   of space and time and song.

The bursting of great colours,
   distract from silent still,
   the nebulas and comets,
   in the universe did fill.

Amazing was the atmosphere,
   the blazing starry host,
Explosions of exuberance,
   The glory and the hope.

REBECCA MOORE

All space was filled with joy,
The news had heard from one,
The knowledge that The Maker,
Had sent His only Son.

The small round planet,
kindly named the apple of His eye,
had fallen to the wicked one,
And they were cursed to die.

The Father's heart was felt by all,
He knew this was the time,
before the earth's creation,
they were always on His mind.

"Now is the time! Now is the time!"
the angel voice did sing,
"Holy Holy is the Lord"
Now to His heart He'll bring.

Each name He crafted on His hands,
Not one would be forgot,
The Great One had His eye on them,
But first it had to cost.

They felt the presence thickly,
The Master passing by,
An awe, an air did fill the space,
The Great One occupied.

PIZZA AND CHOIR

Not usual jubilation,
Happiness and glee,
The universe stood silent,
As they looked towards a tree.

The tree stood tall but haggard,
as it pointed to the sky,
The Favoured One would save the world,
but first He had to die.

And there the Mighty Saviour,
hung upon that tree,
While people jeered and mocked and spat,
—others bended knee.

The universe in agony,
could feel the Father's pain,
The pressure built in atmospheres,
as the Son was slain.

Down came His fist and cracked the earth,
The curtain tore in half,
The thunder rolled, the lightning struck,
Throughout the land was dark.

"Now is the time to finish it,"
The stars could hear His cry,
All power rose within His might,
The earth pulled into line.

The rocks broke open, light shone forth,
The lost released from prison,
"Where has He gone?" the people asked,
—The Son of God has risen!

A joyous shout rang throughout space,
The universe declared:
"The Great and Mighty Son of God
The sins of earth did bare."

How could it be? A love so great,
Could span the space of time?
Before the earth's creation,
You were on His mind.

LIFE IS GOOD

I can count on my hand the number of times when I truly thought I was going to die – and I'm not talking about when I let my husband drive (though he's never had a motor vehicle accident in Australia ... he says)!

One near-death experience was as a teenager when I was caught in a rip while swimming on my boogie-board at the beach. No amount of paddling would move me towards where I wanted to go. So, realising what was happening, I relaxed and let the rip take me where it would, all the while trying to stay calm.

Fortunately, I had my boogie-board to lean on but *unfortunately* the shape of the rip pushed me towards the rocky cliffs of the headland. As the rip curved around, taking me with its flow, each wave threw me closer and closer to the cliff face until I was now so close to the rocks that it suddenly dawned on me that the next wave would probably be my last.

This is it! I thought as I looked in horror at the rocks I was about to be plastered up against. There seemed to be no way out of this situation. As I considered the next wave, I turned to see how far away from me it was. Seemingly out of nowhere a man on a surf board appeared, hand outstretched.

"Need a hand?" he asked.

Immediately I threw my hand into his and he towed me far enough to push me into shore. I never saw him again, but I am so very grateful he was where he was at the time I needed it.

Whether this person was an angel or just happened to be in the right place at the right time, I don't believe it can be put down to a co-incidence or luck. I believe it was God's way of reminding me that His eyes are always on us and if our time is not up, it's not up – we're not yet finished the work that has been predestined for us.

It's a wonderful feeling to know that all the days of our lives are known by God, and to know that we have a purpose and predestined job to do is comforting and hopeful.

Ephesians chapter one verse four says: *"For he chose us in him before the creation of the world to be holy and blameless in his sight. In love he predestined us for adoption to sonship through Jesus Christ, in accordance with his pleasure and will—to the praise of his glorious grace, which he has freely given us in the One he loves."*

This doesn't mean that we are indestructible and can live life recklessly thinking we'll only die when the time is right. There is such a thing as common sense and wisdom which God has deigned to lavish upon us (James chapter 1 verse 5). But, I am grateful that the times I thought were my end, I was given another opportunity to live.

These close calls have made me alert and aware of what a wonderful gift life is. Through moments like these, I have become aware that life can be over in an instant, and that each moment is a treasure to use for the benefit of others and for the glory of the One who made us, who gave us life, and who holds the world in His hands. Therefore, I don't want to waste it.

I write because if my life ended tomorrow, I would want to be sure I took every opportunity to tell the world about the wonderful Father in Heaven who loves us, who sent His Son Jesus to die to redeem us in order to give us the gift of eternal life.

If I don't take every opportunity to show how good our God is, then I have not done my job. I don't want anyone to miss out on His great love. Our lives can be a constant act of worship, as we live in the grace that has been given to us, and share the gift of God's wonderful forgiveness and mercy with others.

I am grateful now for the near-death experiences that I have had, because they gave me the courage to speak and not waste any time.

What are you meant to be doing, and have you begun it? I encourage you to be courageous and bold, and let the time you have in each day be a gift of worship to the One who loves you most.

"Therefore, I urge you, brothers and sisters, in view of God's mercy, to offer your bodies as a living sacrifice, holy and pleasing to God—this is your true and proper worship. Do not conform to the pattern of this world, but be transformed by the renewing of your mind. Then you will be able to test and approve what God's will is—his good, pleasing and perfect will."
—Romans chapter 12 verses 1-2

DON'T BE AFRAID OF SOMETHING NEW

"What?! Only two more sleeps until Christmas?" said every mother who hadn't started her Christmas shopping until the last minute.

That was almost me, but I managed to get my act together in the final few days and, with lots of prayer and minor miracles, no one knew any different (maybe just a little bit). 'Flying by the seat of one's pants' I think it's called.

Thankfully, the task I began was seen through to its completion, even if it was a bit of a close call. More importantly, however, the majority of our family time was spent celebrating the real meaning of Christmas – God with us.

God with us
Now with the new year almost upon us, it is a great time for reflecting upon the completion of one year and celebrating the beginning of a new one. God has brought us through countless events that, if we had known of beforehand, we may have scratched our heads

in concern. But, knowing that God is with us means that, regardless of what the new year brings, we can be assured that God is already there, having gone before us – just as He has in previous years.

"The Lord himself goes before you and will be with you; he will never leave you nor forsake you. Do not be afraid; do not be discouraged."
—Deuteronomy chapter 31 verse 8

His love never fails
His plans for us are good, and while we can't always predict what He has in store for us, we can have peace in that knowledge.

He promises to bring the good work He has begun in us to completion, which means He will not slumber. We are His workmanship, an ongoing work in progress, and I like that. How boring it would be if we already knew everything – no more mysteries to explore and discover. But, instead, we must simply take one step after another knowing that, wherever He leads us, He is the Good Shepherd and we should follow.

"I will instruct you and teach you in the way you should go; I will counsel you with my loving eye on you."
—Psalm chapter 32 verse 8

A big adventure
May this next season be a big adventure for you. May God reveal to you His unknown treasures, and the gifts you never knew existed before, as you carry the wonder, light and joy that your Father in heaven has placed within you to share with those around you.

"This is what the Lord says to his anointed…to open doors before him so that gates will not be shut: I will go before you and will level the mountains; I will break down gates of bronze and cut through bars of iron. I will give you hidden treasures, riches stored in secret places, so that you may know that I am the Lord, the God of Israel, who summons you by name."
—Isaiah chapter 45 verses 1-3

And, in all things, may God's blessings be upon you and yours in the coming days.

AFTERWORD

The hills gently change shape as the clouds nestle in and wrap themselves around each hollow in the valley. The day takes its rest and the wildlife settles for the night. While the world becomes quiet, I take a deep breath, soaking in the beauty of what lies before me. The cool of the night air, the scent of the recently fallen rain, the calling of the birds and the sleepiness only the end of day brings, all send me to a place of sweet serenity.

As I lay my pen down, I cannot help but thank the Lord for all of His blessings. The seasons that have been, the ones that are to come, and in which we now are. I pray we see the beauty in each moment, and are grateful, too, for the growth we find in the trials.

THE END

ABOUT THE AUTHOR

Rebecca lives on the Sunshine Coast, Australia with her husband and four children.

On a rainy day you will find Rebecca wrapped up in a blanket, huddled around a fireplace with a good book, a piano, a cup of hot chocolate and her five most favourite people distracting her from her work.

An internationally published writer and author, publisher and podcaster,
her passion is to inspire others through
words – that capture and present the beauty in life,
love – in the simplicity of everyday moments, and
home – to provide value to being a woman, wife, mother, daughter and friend.

Rebecca's professional goal is to write words
'that bring life, hope and healing, drawing people closer to the light of God, the hope of this world'.
His name is Jesus and He is our home.

ALSO BY REBECCA MOORE

You Could be Dancing
ISBN: 978-0-6484602-1-3
You could be Dancing is the first in the collection of 'short real-world devotionals that make you feel normal' by Christian columnist, wife and mother Rebecca Moore. Rebecca takes you on a journey through 40 inspirational articles and poems about womanhood, life, love and hope, leading you home to where your heart is. Laugh, giggle and cry as Rebecca shares life's journey in a way that makes your life a home, and those you love, its most valued treasures.

Where Rivers Flow
ISBN: 978-0-6453697-6-2
Take a moment to sail down the river with Rebecca as she talks life, love, and the promises of God. The third in the series of 'short real-world devotionals that make you feel normal', *Where Rivers Flow* continues the easy conversation and beautiful poetry that you fell in love with in her first two books *You Could be Dancing* and *Pizza & Choir*. Throughout the book, Rebecca covers topics of walking into your purpose, stepping out of the desert and into your promise. Where Rivers Flow takes you deep into the love of Jesus. You'll find yourself again laughing and reflecting at everyday situations that draw us closer to God and the beauty of home, while drinking in the warmth of her timeless poetry that takes you into another realm. This is the refreshing drink you've been looking for.

The Misty Meadows Children's Series
ISBN: 978-0-6453697-6-2; ISBN: 978-0-6453697-6-2; ISBN: 978-0-6453697-6-2
An inspiring children's series with themes of love, nourishment, growth, patience, and friendship. This is a place best friends come to grow and play and learn to care along the way.

You can find Rebecca online at:
www.rebeccamoore.life; instagram.com/rebeccamoore_author; facebook.com/Rebecca Moore – Author

www.ingramcontent.com/pod-product-compliance
Lightning Source LLC
Chambersburg PA
CBHW032039290426
44110CB00012B/876